NIC BISHOP
SPIDERS

This yellow crab spider is hard to spot on goldenrod flowers. It is waiting to ambush a bee or a butterfly.

NIC BISHOP
SPIDERS

scholastic 💡 nonfiction

an imprint of

📖 SCHOLASTIC

LIBRARY OF CONGRESS CATALOGING-IN-PUBLICATION DATA
Bishop, Nic, 1955- • Nic Bishop spiders / Nic Bishop. • p. cm. • 1. Spiders—Juvenile
literature. 2. Spiders—Pictorial works—Juvenile literature. • I. Title. • QL458.4.B58 •
2007 • 595.4'4—dc22 • 2006047179

ISBN 13: 978-0-439-87756-5 • ISBN 10: 0-439-87756-3

10 9 8 7 6 5 4 3 2 1   07 08 09 10 11

Printed in Singapore   46
First printing, September 2007
Book design by Nancy Sabato

To Sam, with thanks

—N. B.

SPIDERS were hunting long before lions and tigers. They were hunting even before *Tyrannosaurus rex.*

They were one of the first predators to walk on land, starting more than 350 million years ago. And they are still one of the most successful predators. Today, there are more than 38,000 types of spiders. They live almost everywhere, even in your basement.

The green lynx spider hunts for insects in fields, parks, and even backyards.

Some spiders are as small as a grain of sand. **The biggest, the Goliath birdeater tarantula from South America, is as big as a page in this book.** Yet all spiders share similar features. They have eight legs, fangs, spin silk, and eat other animals. At first you might confuse them with insects. But it is easy to tell the difference. Insects have six legs; spiders have eight. And spiders never have wings.

The Goliath birdeater tarantula likes to stay near its burrow on the rain forest floor. It waits for prey to come close enough to grab.

A spider's body has two main parts.

The back part is called the abdomen. This contains the heart, which pumps pale blue blood (yes, blue!), and the spinnerets, which make silk. The front, or head part is called the cephalothorax. It has the spider's legs, eyes, fangs, brain, stomach, and two short arms, called pedipalps, which a spider uses to hold its prey.

The green lynx spider is perfectly camouflaged when it hides among leaves waiting to pounce on an insect. The long black spines on its legs are thought to help it trap its prey.

Spiders eat in an unusual way. They don't chew and swallow food like you do. They drink it. **First the spider stabs its prey with its fangs and injects poisonous venom to stop it from moving.** Then it dribbles digestive juices on its meal. This turns the animal's insides into soup, so the spider can slurp them out. Afterward, all that's left of the prey are empty bits of skin and some wings.

This black widow spider has just caught a wasp in her web. She will feed once she has wrapped it safely in silk.

Most spiders have eight eyes, so they can look several ways at once. But a spider cannot see as clearly as you. Their eyes are usually very small and simple. Spiders will notice if something moves nearby, but they often cannot see shapes very well.

A few spiders have no eyes at all. They live deep inside caves where it is completely dark all the time. But they have no trouble catching prey. That's because spiders have other amazing senses to rely on.

The long-jawed spider is a web builder. It gets its name from the very long jaws that hold the two thin fangs, which you can see folded underneath.

A spider does not have a nose or ears, at least not like you do. Even so, it has extraordinary senses all over its body. Take a close look. You will see this spider is covered with hairs. Many of these sense touch, vibrations, and sounds.

Hairs on a spider's legs can sense the sound of a flying insect.

Other organs on the feet can smell and taste things just by walking on them. A spider can even recognize the taste of its own silk by touching it.

This huntsman spider is beautifully camouflaged on a rain forest leaf. Hairs on its body and legs will sense the vibrations made by the footsteps of an approaching insect.

Spider skin is made of tough stuff called chitin. It is the spider's personal body armor as well as its skeleton. Spiders don't have bones inside their body for support. Their hard skin is like a skeleton they wear on the outside. It protects and supports the spider's body.

This hard skin does not stretch, so a spider must molt now and then as it grows. **The spider finds a safe place and then slowly squeezes out of its old skin.** It can take an hour and is very stressful. The spider must even shed the skin covering its eyes and the inside of its mouth. Afterward, its new skin is damp and soft like putty. The spider rests until its new skin dries and hardens.

A cobalt-blue tarantula has to roll onto its back to molt. It is pulling the old skin off its legs. Its new fangs are pure white, but will turn dark later.

Silk is the secret of spider success. Spiders make several different types, which can be sticky, stretchy, strong, or fluffy. Each has a special use: for making egg sacs, wrapping prey, building webs, or making draglines that the spider trails as it walks along or jumps.

Silk is made by the spinnerets on the spider's abdomen. Liquid threads come out of dozens of tiny nozzles and turn solid as the spider pulls them. Spider silk is an amazing substance. It can be stronger than steel and can stretch twice its own length. Best of all, it's recyclable. A spider can eat its silk when it has finished with it.

A black-and-yellow garden spider will use its legs to turn its prey as it wraps it with silk from its spinnerets.

Spiderwebs are made of silk. Some webs look like old tissue paper draped on hedges. Others hang in messy tangles in the corner of your garage. But the best known is the orb web with its wonderful spiral of sticky threads. A large orb web may contain more than 100 feet of silk thread and can take about an hour to build.

Most spiders build their webs at night, working by touch. Once finished, the spider sits in the middle or at the edge and holds the web so it can feel the vibration of a trapped insect. If the prey is a dangerous wasp, the spider may cut it free. Otherwise it wraps the prey in silk and bites.

Orb web spiders have special claws and non-stick feet so they can walk on their webs without getting stuck.

Many spiders don't use webs. They hunt prey instead. Each type of spider looks for food in a different place. Wolf spiders prowl in leaf litter at night. They have large eyes and sense vibrations to find prey. **Fishing spiders rest at the water's edge with one foot on the surface.** They feel for the tiny ripples made by an insect that has fallen in or a tadpole swimming close to the surface. Then they rush over the surface to bite it. Lynx spiders like to hunt in leafy, green, weedy places. They have good eyesight and pounce on insects. Some lynx spiders even spit venom at their enemies.

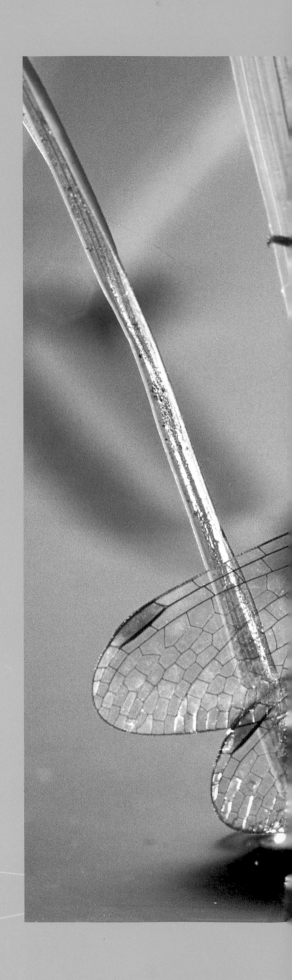

This fishing spider has just caught a dragonfly that crashed into the water nearby.

Then it *pounces*!

A jumping spider can leap twenty times its body length. That is like you jumping 80 feet!

A jumping spider always trails a dragline when it leaps. If it misses its target, the spider can climb back to where it started.

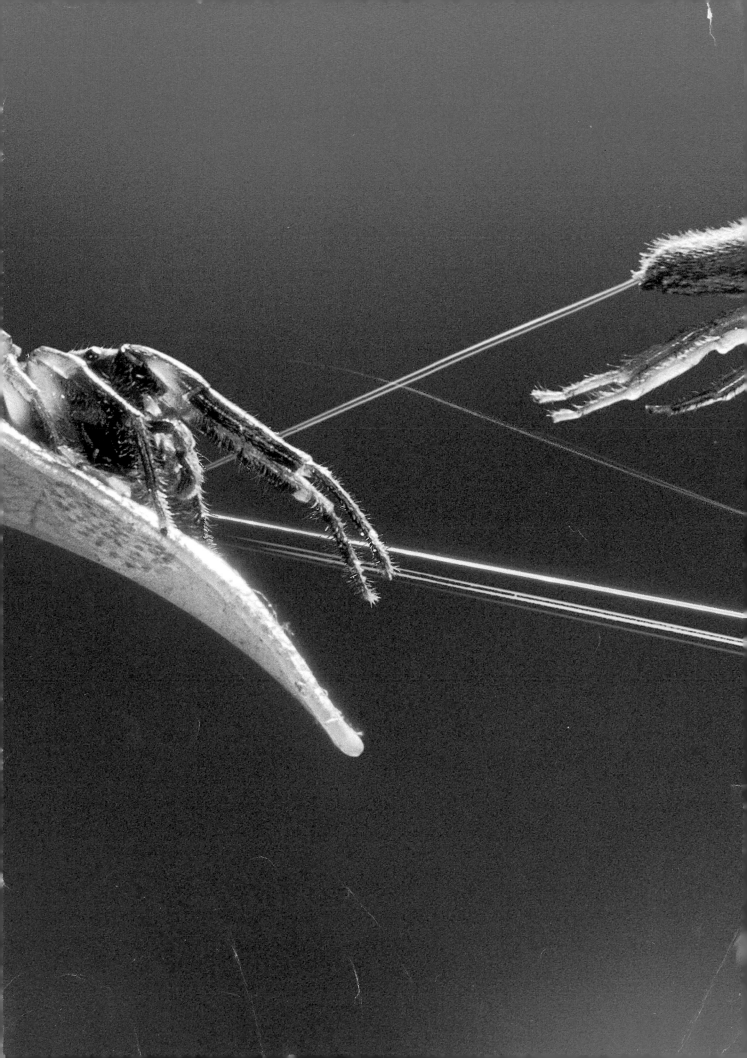

Jumping spiders have the best sight of any kind of spider. You can often find them exploring tree trunks and leaves, looking for anything that moves. When it spots something, the spider creeps closer, like a cat, for a better look.

Its two large eyes work like binoculars to recognize prey. The two smaller ones on each side work out how far it needs to jump.

Jumping spiders are easy to recognize because of their big eyes. You often find them in backyards, and sometimes they even come indoors.

Tarantulas are the kings and queens of ambush. At night they sit in the entrances of their dens, waiting for something tasty to walk by. It might be a cockroach or a frog. Even a mouse will do because tarantulas are the biggest spiders of all. Tarantulas are different in other ways, too. **While most spiders live only a year or two, some tarantulas can live for thirty years.** Tarantulas have fangs that bite downward like a snake's. Other spiders have fangs that bite sideways like pincers.

A huge cockroach is the perfect meal for a rose-hair tarantula.

All spiders have enemies, even tarantulas. Giant wasps, called tarantula hawks, find tarantulas in their dens. The wasps sting them and use them as food for their young. Birds, lizards, centipedes, and scorpions also eat spiders.

A few spiders defend themselves by trying to bite. Some tarantulas brush hairs, like tiny darts, from their body. These stick and sting in the eyes and nose of their attacker. **But most spiders are not as fierce as you think.** They would rather run and hide. A web spider may drop to the ground on a long silk thread, then climb back up when danger has passed. Many spiders look like bark or even bird droppings so they won't be noticed.

Some tarantulas rear up and show off their fangs to scare enemies.

The most dangerous time for a male spider is when he looks for a mate.

He has to watch out for other males that may fight or chase him. These two male jumping spiders are trying to scare

each other by showing off their fangs and holding
their front legs out wide. At the same time, they run
sideways and back and forth, like dancing crabs.
Eventually one of them will run under the leaf to hide.

Male spiders may threaten each other
if they meet. The smaller one will often
run for safety to avoid a serious fight.

This jumping spider is dancing on tiptoes. When he gets close, he touches the female to see if she will let him mate.

The real danger starts when the male spots a female. She is often bigger than he is and may want to eat him. He finds the female by following her silk. Each spider foot can taste the silk of a female because she coats it with a special chemical called a pheromone. Now he just needs to make sure she doesn't think he is a meal. Spiders do not have a voice box so they cannot sing or call to each other. They communicate in other ways.

The male spider may tap the ground, wiggle his pedipalps with excitement, or pluck her web with a special signal. **Jumping spiders dance for a female.** The male often waves his legs as if to say, "Don't eat me, I can be your mate." The female may signal back if she recognizes him. Then he comes closer, doing his dance but always ready to run off if necessary.

After mating, the female lays her eggs on a fresh silk sheet. **Some spiders lay a handful of eggs, and others lay more than 2,000.** Then she spins a silk cover until she has a secure egg sac. She may leave the egg sac hidden in a safe spot. Or if she is a jumping spider or a crab spider, she will guard the egg sac. Wolf spiders carry their egg sacs, even when they hunt.

A female wolf spider carries her egg sac attached to the spinnerets. She will go back to find the egg sac if it falls off.

When they are ready, the spiderlings chew their way out of their egg sac, sometimes with help from their mother. They look like miniature adults and soon wander off to look after themselves. Only a few spiders look after their babies. **The wolf spider will carry her young on her back for a few days.** A spider called a mothercare spider feeds its babies with "spider milk" from its mouth. Some tarantulas share food with their spiderlings.

Wolf spider young cling to their mother's back. She will let them climb up her legs if they tumble off.

But eventually all young will leave to find new places to live. Many spiderlings have a clever way of doing this. They use their silk to fly. The spiderlings climb to the tops of twigs and leaves. Then they let out long streamers of silk until the breeze catches and carries them into the sky. Some will only sail for a few yards. But others may float on the wind for more than 100 miles.

This spiderling is searching for its first meal in a miniature forest of moss plants. It is barely larger than two poppy seeds now. It will grow about one thousand times bigger by the time it is an adult.

I go on some interesting expeditions in search of my subjects.

I have visited the rain forests of French Guiana and Costa Rica to look for tarantulas. In New Guinea I once saw groups of spiders that spun webs big enough to trap large birds. The local people told me that they wind the sheets of silk onto branches to make bags. Then they roast the spiders for snacks.

One of my favorite spider trips was to Florida. My wife and I spent a week there looking for an ogre-faced spider. It has large eyes like an owl and comes out after dark. It spins a small web and holds it like a fishing net to trap insects. We searched for hours in swamps, forests, and along roads, but we never found one. Even so, we were not disappointed because we saw so many other amazing things. At night the forest shines with wonderful webs of every kind, and wolf spiders as big as your hand prowl across the forest floor. We watched armadillos feeding and listened to alligators calling.

Several spiders in this book were raised at home. I watched over them for months as they grew up, so I could photograph rare events like molting, courting, or egg-laying.

My list of spider houseguests included crab spiders, jumping spiders, and wolf spiders. One particularly big spider learned to push open the lid of its cage and wanted to build a home behind the bookcase. Another ended up on the ceiling. But everyone else was well behaved. A few spiders even went on holiday with me, if they needed special care. It's lucky they do not take up much room and that my wife is very understanding.

You have to be quiet when photographing spiders, otherwise they will think you are a predator and want to hide. The most complicated photograph

I took for this book was of the jumping spider in action. I used a sensitive laser beam to fire the camera when the spider jumped. I also used a hand-built shutter that opens very fast and several specially-built flashguns to freeze the action on film.

To capture each stage of the spider jump, I moved the laser beam a little every time I took a photograph. Then I used a computer to put the photographs together. The spider had to jump many times for me to get the right shots. But we took a break now and then so I could give the spider a drink of water and a fly for a snack.

For more information about Nic Bishop, go to www.nicbishop.com.

Index

Entries in **bold** indicate photographs.

Glossary

Dragline A strong, stiff strand of silk produced by a spider. The spider uses it to form the framework of its web and as a way of lowering and raising itself.

Molt To periodically shed an outer layer, such as skin, shell, hair, feathers, or horns.

Predator An animal that lives by hunting other animals for food.

Prey An animal that is hunted by another animal for food.

Spiderling Newborn spider.

Venom Poison produced by some snakes and spiders. Venom usually passes into the victim's body through a bite or sting.